# SKILL BUILDER
# GRAMMAR

LEVEL
**1**

PUFFIN BOOKS

An imprint of Penguin Random House

## PUFFIN BOOKS

USA | Canada | UK | Ireland | Australia
New Zealand | India | South Africa | China

Puffin Books is part of the Penguin Random House group of companies
whose addresses can be found at global.penguinrandomhouse.com

Published by Penguin Random House India Pvt. Ltd
7th Floor, Infinity Tower C, DLF Cyber City,
Gurgaon 122 002, Haryana, India

First published in Puffin Books by Penguin Random House India 2021

Text, design and illustrations copyright © Quadrum Solutions Pvt. Ltd 2021
Series copyright © Penguin Random House India 2021

All rights reserved

10 9 8 7 6 5 4 3 2 1

ISBN 9780143445036

Design and layout by Quadrum Solutions Pvt. Ltd
Printed at Aarvee Promotions, India

www.penguin.co.in

# Dear Moms and Dads,

There's no better way to prepare your children for their future than to equip them with all the skills they need to grow into confident adults. The Skill Builder series has been created to hone subject skills as well as twenty-first century skills so that children develop not just academic skills but also life skills.

The books in the Skill Builder series focus on numerical, science and English language skills. Recognizing that children learn best while having fun, the books in this series have been created with a high 'fun' quotient. Each subject is dealt with across four levels, so you can choose the level that best suits your child's learning stage.

The Skill Builder: Grammar books have been created by academic experts who have devised a special chart to help you track the skills your child needs to master in order to understand and apply grammatical concepts.

It has been great creating this series with my highly charged Quadrum team—our academic experts, Krupa Shah and Naimisha Sanghavi, who spent hours crafting each page; Himani, who designed every page to be a visual treat; Gopi, who painstakingly laid out every word; Bishnupriya and Ruby, who read and reread every word; and Kunjli, who was the conscience of the entire series. And of course, the Puffin team—Sohini and Ashwitha— who added value at every step. When you have a great team, you're bound to have a great book.

I do hope you and your child enjoy the series as much as we have enjoyed creating it.

## Sonia Mehta
PS: We'd love your feedback, so do write in to us at
**funlearningbooks@quadrumltd.com**

# THE SKILL CHART

Here's a snapshot of the skills your child will acquire as they complete the activities:

- **Reading skills:** The ability to read and comprehend text with proficiency.
- **Writing skills:** The ability to form meaningful sentences and write with proficiency.
- **Speaking skills:** The ability to speak fluently and proficiently in the English language.
- **Punctuation skills:** The ability to use punctuation marks in the correct manner so as to form meaningful sentences.
- **Creative thinking skills:** The ability to view a problem creatively from different angles.
- **Decision-making skills:** The ability to choose between possible solutions to a problem, through an intuitive or reasoned process, or both.
- **Critical thinking/problem-solving skills:** Rationalizing, analysing, evaluating and interpreting information to make informed judgements.

| Page no. | | Reading | Writing | Speaking | Punctuation | Creative thinking | Decision-making | Problem-solving/Critical thinking |
|---|---|---|---|---|---|---|---|---|
| 4 | CIRCLE IT | | ☺ | ☺ | | | | |
| 5 | NOUN CIRCLES | | ☺ | ☺ | | | | |
| 6 | WHAT WILL YOU BE? | | ☺ | | | | ☺ | |
| 7 | PICTURE TALK | | ☺ | | | ☺ | | |
| 8 | CIRCLE AND REWRITE | ☺ | | | ☺ | | | ☺ |
| 9 | FILL IT UP | | | | ☺ | | | ☺ |
| 10 | BLOOMING NOUNS | | ☺ | | | ☺ | ☺ | |
| 11 | NOUN STORY | ☺ | | | ☺ | | | ☺ |
| 12 | CAPITAL TIME | ☺ | | | ☺ | | | ☺ |
| 13 | CAPITAL LETTERS | ☺ | | | ☺ | | | ☺ |
| 14 | ANSWER ME | ☺ | ☺ | ☺ | ☺ | | ☺ | |
| 15 | TO MARKET, TO MARKET | ☺ | | ☺ | | | | |
| 16 | HOOT HOOT | | ☺ | ☺ | ☺ | ☺ | | |
| 18 | WHO LIKES CUPCAKES? | | | | ☺ | | ☺ | ☺ |
| 19 | REVERSE PRONOUNS | ☺ | | | | | ☺ | ☺ |
| 20 | CAR PARK | | | | | ☺ | | ☺ |

# CIRCLE IT

Circle the correct article to be used with each word.

Tip: **A**, **an** and **the** are called articles.

| a umbrella | an umbrella |
|---|---|

| a table | an table |
|---|---|

| a octopus | an octopus |
|---|---|

| a basket | an basket |
|---|---|

| a train | an train |
|---|---|

| a puppy | an puppy |
|---|---|

# NOUN CIRCLES

Colour the circles containing nouns that take the article **a** in yellow. Colour the circles containing nouns that take the article **an** in blue.

# WHAT WILL YOU BE?

Look at the pictures and complete the sentences below.

Hint: Remember to use the articles **a** or **an**.

astronaut     singer     sailor     doctor

I would like to be

_____ _____

when I grow up.

I would like to be

_____ _____

when I grow up.

I would like to be

_____ _____

when I grow up.

I would like to be

_____ _____

when I grow up.

Write five sentences about the picture below. Remember to use the articles **a** and **an** in your sentences.

_____

_____

_____

_____

_____

_____

_____

_____

_____

_____

# CIRCLE AND REWRITE

Circle the proper nouns below. Then, rewrite each using a capital letter.

Tip: Common nouns are general names for people, places, animals or things. Proper nouns are specific names for people, places, organizations or things.

mr kapoor

wednesday

movie

june

china

teacher

sister

ray's pizza

cafe

building

banana

month

cartoon

balloon

mumbai

# FILL IT UP

Add appropriate common or proper nouns to the table below. One has been done for you.

| Common noun | Proper noun |
| --- | --- |
| dog | Trixie |
| park | |
| | Yamuna |
| | New York |
| restaurant | |
| book | |
| school | |
| | Eiffel Tower |
| boy | |

# BLOOMING NOUNS

Fill up the petals of the blue-centred flower with common nouns and the petals of the purple-centred flower with proper nouns.

Write an interesting story using at least three common nouns and at least two proper nouns from the box.

Shanghai    bus    wheel    pencil    box
Rahim    Nita    Everest    book    glasses

# CAPITAL TIME

Circle the word in each group that should start with a capital letter.

1. boy      ricky      son

2. city      country      chicago

3. tuesday      week      day

4. river      water      ganges

5. indian      people      country

6. food      sandwich      brussels sprout

7. me      you      i

8. monument      taj mahal      wonder

Read the sentences below and rewrite them using capital letters in the right places.

1   tara's birthday is on tuesday.

_____

2   i like her red purse.

_____

3   anita and i can speak spanish.

_____

4   he lives in the city of sydney in australia.

_____

# ANSWER ME

Answer the following questions in complete sentences. Use capital letters in the right places.

1   What is your mother's name?

_____

2   Who are your neighbours?

_____

3   What is your favourite colour?

_____

4   When is your birthday?

_____

5   What is the name of your school?

_____

# TO MARKET, TO MARKET

Tia wrote to her friend about her trip to the local market with her parents. Help her out by rewriting her letter using capital letters in the right places.

hello sandhya,

how are you Doing? today, i went to the market with Mum and Dad. there were a lot of Shops there. there was a Florist called petals, who had lovely fresh Flowers of all kinds.
there was also a Vegetable vendor who had Lots of vegetables like Broccoli, cherry tomatoes and bell peppers. there were a lot of people, so my mum told me to hold her hand and not to wander off.
we are going back next friday to buy more Groceries. i'm looking forward to it.

love,
tia

# HOOT HOOT

Look at each picture carefully. Then, write a sentence about it using one or more words from the box.

Two have been done for you.

> I    we    you    he
>
> she    they    it

1. I am an owl.

2. You are a child.

3

4

5

6

7

17

# WHO LIKES CUPCAKES?

Replace the underlined nouns with pronouns from the box.

we     it     she     he

1  <u>Dad and I</u> got some cupcakes.

_____

2  <u>The blueberry cupcake</u> was my favourite.

_____

3  <u>My friend Lina</u> ate the vanilla cupcake.

_____

4  <u>Harry</u> doesn't like cupcakes.

_____

5  <u>Mum</u> enjoyed the dark chocolate cupcake.

_____

# REVERSE PRONOUNS

Read the sentences below and circle the pronoun in each sentence. Then, write a noun in the box that could replace the pronoun.

1. He was wearing a cap.

2. It was in the box.

3. They were going to the park.

4. She dances very well.

5. We like to read mystery novels.

6. They finished all the water.

19

# CAR PARK

Colour the cars that contain action words in orange.

cat

tank

radio

yell

knit

jump

talk

sing

shelf

bottle

turn

bake

# ANIMAL ACTIONS

Match each action word to the correct picture.

  •                    •  flying

  •                    •  hopping

  •                    •  swimming

  •                    •  eating

  •                    •  licking

# FILL IN THE ACTIONS

Read the sentences below and fill in the blanks with appropriate action words.

Tip: Action words are also called verbs.

1    Grandma will _____ a scarf for me.

2    Jay _____ the dishes every night.

3    Seema will _____ the box
     to the post office.

4    We _____ tennis on Saturdays.

5    Mira was _____ a book.

6    Dad _____ his mother every day.

7    The leaves of this tree _____ yellow in
     the autumn.

8    They _____ their dinner at 7.00 p.m.

# VERB SORT

Sort the verbs from the box by writing them in the correct columns of the table below.

run    will walk    opened    will go

smelled    call    jogged    fly

cooked    will drink    copy    will sing

| Past tense | Present tense | Future tense |
|------------|---------------|--------------|
|            |               |              |
|            |               |              |
|            |               |              |
|            |               |              |

# CIRCLE TIME

Read the sentences below and circle all the describing words you can find.

1   The car was very fast.

2   I ate a red apple.

3   There are seven members in my family.

4   A big bird flew by.

5   Dad was wearing a striped shirt.

6   I gave Mum a tight hug.

7   I saw a beautiful butterfly.

8   I ate a crunchy cucumber.

# SORT IT

Write each describing word in the correct column.

Tip: Describing words are called adjectives.

triangular

star-shaped

tiny

bad

green

new

round

tall

five-year-old

beautiful

bright

red

amazing

young

enormous

| Size | Shape | Age | Colour | Opinion |
|------|-------|-----|--------|---------|
|      |       |     |        |         |
|      |       |     |        |         |
|      |       |     |        |         |

# PICTURE ADJECTIVES

Write two sentences using a different adjective in each to describe each picture below.

_____

_____

_____

_____

_____

_____

# WHERE'S THE MOUSE?

Match each picture with the word or words that best describe the position of the mouse.

Tip: Prepositions show the relationship between the words in a sentence.

in •

on •

under •

behind •

in front of •

between •

# FILL IT IN

Complete each sentence using a preposition from the box.

| from | until | off | about | at | against | over |

1. The old lady got _____ the bus carefully.

2. Srinath was the only one _____ the beach.

3. The frog jumped _____ the log.

4. Wanda leaned _____ the wall.

5. Wait _____ after dinner for dessert.

6. The movie was _____ a faithful dog.

7. We ran home _____ school.

# FLEA MARKET

Look at the image below and write six sentences about it. Each sentence should contain a different preposition. Here are some prepositions you could use:

> in    on    off    besides    between
> in front of    behind    opposite    next to

1 _____

_____

2 _____

_____

3 _____

_____

4 _____

_____

5 _____

_____

6 _____

_____

# MATCH THE OPPOSITES

Draw a line to connect each word to its opposite.

soft　　　day　　　happy　　　full　　　fast　　　hot

cold　　empty　　　slow　　　night　　　sad　　　hard

# WRITE THE OPPOSITE

Write the opposites of the following words.

| | | | |
|---|---|---|---|
| up | | dirty | |
| low | | few | |
| heavy | | awake | |
| finish | | early | |
| thick | | open | |

# FLOWER POWER

Say whether the nouns below are masculine, feminine or common and write them out on the petals of the correct flower.

nun

citizen

king

daughter

princess

spouse

Feminine

Common

niece

artist

father

uncle

infant

grandson

aunt

vixen

parent

child

lion

wizard

teacher

groom

author

hen

grandma

Masculine

nephew

# WHICH TENSE?

Colour the box that identifies the tense of each sentence correctly.

1  We went to the zoo.

| past tense | present tense | future tense |

2  Rita likes chocolate ice cream.

| past tense | present tense | future tense |

3  Mum will go to the market tomorrow.

| past tense | present tense | future tense |

4  Dad wore a blue shirt yesterday.

| past tense | present tense | future tense |

5  He will make pancakes for breakfast.

| past tense | present tense | future tense |

Fill in the blanks using verbs in the tenses indicated.

1   Wei _____ in Tokyo. live; present

2   Dad _____ a doll's house for me.
    build; future

3   I _____ a book before bedtime.
    read; present

4   The dog _____ at the milkman.
    bark; present

5   He _____ the lawn on Saturday.
    mow; future

6   Mona _____ a snowman. build; future

7   The train _____ here for a couple of
    minutes.  stop; present

# IN THE PAST

Fill in the blanks with the past tense forms of the highlighted verbs.

1. They _____ on a family holiday. go

2. He _____ two glasses of juice. drink

3. She _____ her parents to the mall. drive

4. I _____ home from the park. run

5. They _____ for an hour. swim

6. Tom _____ Alberto at school. meet

7. He _____ the glass table. break

# TENSE SENTENCE

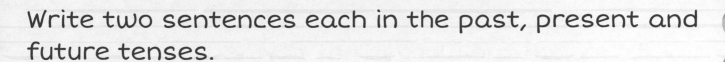

Write two sentences each in the past, present and future tenses.

## Past tense

_____

_____

## Present tense

_____

_____

## Future tense

_____

_____

# MATCH THE RHYME

Name the pictures below out loud. Then, draw a line to match the words that rhyme.

# WHAT'S THE RHYME?

Complete each sentence using a word that rhymes with the highlighted word.

1   There are _____ people in my family.
    fix

2   She fell down and fractured her _____.
    band

3   They declared Vicky the _____. dinner

4   I got eight _____ for my birthday. lifts

5   Please open the _____. floor

6   Turn to _____ 15. sage

7   We saw a big mango _____. free

# IS IT AN ADVERB?

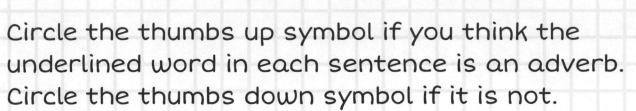

Circle the thumbs up symbol if you think the underlined word in each sentence is an adverb. Circle the thumbs down symbol if it is not.

Tip: An adverb describes the action word or verb in a sentence.

1   Neel is a <u>tall</u> boy.

2   Rita read her book <u>silently</u>.

3   David finished his work <u>quickly</u>.

4   The bunny went <u>hopping</u> in the bushes.

5   Tia <u>sleepily</u> ate her dinner.

6   My teacher <u>drew</u> an apple on the board.

# CIRCLE THE ADVERBS

Read the sentences below and circle all the adverbs you can find.

1   We sang happily at the party.

2   Mahesh blew up the balloon quickly.

3   She opened her gifts carefully.

4   I go to school daily.

5   We went outside after dinner.

6   Breakfast will be ready soon.

7   The toys are lying about everywhere.

# FILL IN THE ADVERBS

Fill in the blanks with appropriate adverbs.

1   The tiger moved _____.

2   Papa carries the baby _____.

3   Sia entered the class _____.

4   Tina played the drum _____.

5   Sam slides _____.

6   Dad painted the picture _____.

7   She skipped around _____.

8   Karim fought the battle _____.

9   Lila sang _____.

10   The children waited for the cake _____.

# ADVERB SENTENCES

Write a sentence using each adverb below.

1 rapidly

_____

2 often

_____

3 honestly

_____

4 nearby

_____

5 nicely

_____

# SYNONYM MATCH

Draw a line to connect words that have similar meanings. Tip: Synonyms are words that have the same or similar meanings.

| | |
|---|---|
| small | damp |
| cost | glad |
| funny | hilarious |
| happy | ill |
| mix | blend |
| sick | child |
| kid | price |
| mistake | error |
| wet | tiny |

# REPLACE THE SYNONYMS

Rewrite each sentence using a synonym for the underlined word.

1    Uncle Jack got me a big birthday <u>gift</u>.

_____

2    This looks difficult, but it is actually <u>simple</u> to understand.

_____

3    The elephant is a <u>big</u> animal.

_____

4    Please <u>shut</u> the windows.

_____

# PUNCTUATION FUN

Add the right punctuation mark to the end of each sentence.

Remember: Declarative sentences (ending in '.') are statements. Exclamatory sentences (ending in '!') indicate strong feelings. Imperative sentences (ending in '.' or '!') are commands, orders, requests or directions. Interrogative sentences (ending in '?') ask questions.

1   Did you finish reading the book ☐

2   Come here right now ☐

3   What a beautiful day it is ☐

4   The table is brown ☐

5   Can we go get an ice cream ☐

6   Stop doing that ☐

7   I can't wait to go on holiday ☐

8   The mangoes are very sweet ☐

9    Go to your room

10   We won

11   What time is the concert

12   My bunny likes to eat carrots

Now write two sentences each that end with a (.),
a (?) or a (!).

_____

_____

_____

_____

_____

# READ AND COLOUR

Read these sentences. Colour the box that identifies the type of sentence each one is.

How old is your sister?

| declarative | imperative | exclamatory | interrogative |

Mom got me a big ball.

| declarative | imperative | exclamatory | interrogative |

That is not fair!

| declarative | imperative | exclamatory | interrogative |

Go and sit there.

| declarative | imperative | exclamatory | interrogative |

# MAKE SENTENCES

Look at the picture below and write one sentence
of each type that describes it.

Declarative

_____

Imperative

_____

Exclamatory

_____

Interrogative

_____

# PUNCTUATION MATCH

Match each description to the punctuation mark it describes. One has been done for you.

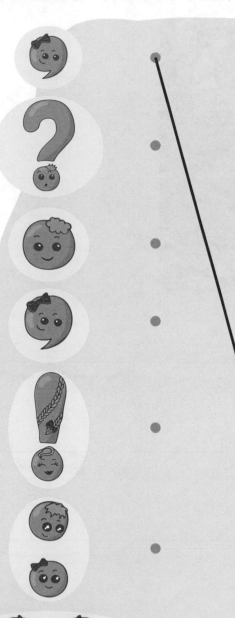

- Used to show the end of sentence
- Used to separate items in a list
- Used to show that a question is being asked
- Used to show strong feeling or emphasis
- Used to show that something is being said
- Used to introduce a list
- Used to show ownership

# SAYING IT RIGHT

Rewrite each sentence using capital letters and punctuation wherever needed.

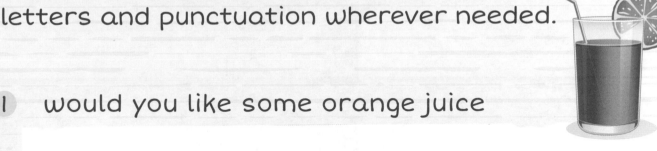

1. would you like some orange juice

_____

2. my parents got me a ball two pencils a box of crayons and a bottle

_____

3. ouch the pan is hot

_____

4. mom said go give this to grandma

_____

# SINGULAR OR PLURAL?

Say whether the words below are singular or plural.

| box | | cap | |
|---|---|---|---|

| log | | eggs | |
|---|---|---|---|

| boys | | monkey | |
|---|---|---|---|

| apples | | lilies | |
|---|---|---|---|

| sock | | shoes | |
|---|---|---|---|

| bottles | | eraser | |
|---|---|---|---|

| bus | | toy | |
|---|---|---|---|

# WRITE THE WORD

Look at each pair of pictures. Write the singular and plural words for each pair.

1.

2.

3.

4.

# PLAYTIME

Write six sentences about this picture. Underline the singular words in red and the plural words in blue.

56

1 _____

_____

2 _____

_____

3 _____

_____

4 _____

_____

5 _____

_____

6 _____

_____

# FILL THE CONJUNCTIONS

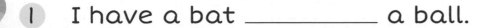

Fill in the blanks using **and, or, but**.
Tip: Conjunctions are used to connect two words, phrases or sentences.

1  I have a bat _____ a ball.

2  I know Jill _____ not her brother.

3  Would you like some cake _____ some ice cream?

4  I want to visit Grandpa _____ he lives too far away for me to go on my own.

5  You may read a book _____ you may go out and play.

6  We ironed the clothes _____ put them in the cupboard.

# JOINT SENTENCES

Write your own sentences using the sets of words given below.

1    apple, banana, or

_____

2    dog, cat, but

_____

3    balloon, ball, and

_____

4    cheese, bread, but

_____

5    spoon, fork, or

_____

# ANSWERS

## page 4 CIRCLE IT
Boxes to be circled: an umbrella, a table, an octopus, a basket, a train, a puppy

## page 5 NOUN CIRCLES

## page 6 WHAT WILL YOU BE?
a singer, an astronaut,
a sailor, a doctor

## page 7 PICTURE TALK
Answers will vary.

## page 8 CIRCLE AND REWRITE
Words to be circled and rewritten: Mr Kapoor, June, Wednesday, China, Ray's Pizza, Mumbai

## page 9 FILL IT UP
Some possible answers:

| Common noun | Proper noun |
|---|---|
| dog | Trixie |
| park | Central Park |
| river | Yamuna |
| city | New York |
| restaurant | Asian Palace |
| book | The Wizard of Oz |
| school | New English School |
| monument | Eiffel Tower |
| boy | Mahesh |

## page 10 BLOOMING NOUNS
Answers will vary.

## page 11 NOUN STORY
Answers will vary.

## page 12 CAPITAL TIME
1. Ricky  2. Chicago  3. Tuesday  4. Ganges  5. Indian
6. Brussels sprout  7. I  8. Taj Mahal

## page 13 CAPITAL LETTERS
1. Tara's birthday is on Tuesday. 2. I like her red purse. 3. Anita and I can speak Spanish. 4. He lives in the city of Sydney in Australia.

## page 14 ANSWER ME
Answers will vary.

## page 15 TO MARKET, TO MARKET
Hello Sandhya,

How are you doing? Today, I went to the market with Mum and Dad. There were a lot of shops there. There was a florist called Petals, who had lovely fresh flowers of all kinds.
There was also a vegetable vendor who had lots of vegetables like broccoli, cherry tomatoes and bell peppers. There were a lot of people, so my mum told me to hold her hand and not to wander off.
We are going back next Friday to buy more groceries. I'm looking forward to it.

Love,
Tia

## pages 16–17 HOOT HOOT
3. It is not an owl. OR It is a block.
4. He is an owl.     5. We are owls.
6. They are owls.   7. She is an owl.

## page 18 WHO LIKES CUPCAKES?
1. We got some cupcakes. 2. It was my favourite.
3. She ate the vanilla cupcake. 4. He doesn't like cupcakes.
5. She enjoyed the dark chocolate cupcake.

## page 19 REVERSE PRONOUNS
Pronouns: 1. He, 2. It, 3. They, 4. She, 5. We, 6. They;
Nouns will vary.

## page 20 CAR PARK
Cars to be coloured: yell, jump, knit, talk, sing, turn, bake

## page 21 ANIMAL ACTIONS

**page 22 FILL IN THE ACTIONS**
1. knit, 2. washes, 3. take, 4. play, 5. reading, 6. calls, 7. turn, 8. eat

**page 23 VERB SORT**
Past tense: jogged, opened, smelled, cooked
Present tense: run, fly, call, copy
Future tense: will drink, will sing, will walk, will go

**page 24 CIRCLE TIME**
1. fast, 2. red, 3. seven, 4. big, 5. striped, 6. tight, 7. beautiful, 8. crunchy

**page 25 SORT IT**

| Size | Shape | Age | Colour | Opinion |
| --- | --- | --- | --- | --- |
| tiny | triangular | five-year-old | bright | amazing |
| enormous | round | young | red | bad |
| tall | star-shaped | new | green | beautiful |

**pages 26–27 PICTURE ADJECTIVES**
Answers will vary.

**page 28 WHERE'S THE MOUSE?**

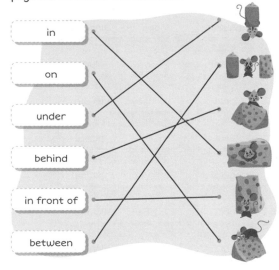

**page 29 FILL IT IN**
1. off, 2. at, 3. over, 4. against, 5. until, 6. about, 7. from

**pages 30–31 FLEA MARKET**
Answers will vary.

**page 32 MATCH THE OPPOSITES**

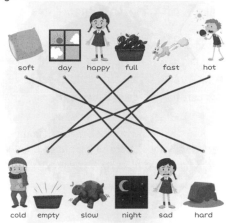

**page 33 WRITE THE OPPOSITE**
down, clean, high, many, light, asleep, start, late, thin, close

**pages 34–35 FLOWER POWER**
Feminine: nun, daughter, princess, niece, aunt, vixen, hen, grandma

Common: citizen, spouse, author, artist, child, infant, parent, teacher

Masculine: king, uncle, wizard, father, grandson, lion, groom, nephew

**page 36 WHICH TENSE?**
1. past tense, 2. present tense, 3. future tense, 4. past tense, 5. future tense

**page 37 COMPLETE ME**
1. lives, 2. will build, 3. read, 4. barks, 5. will mow, 6. will build, 7. stops

**page 38 IN THE PAST**
1. went, 2. drank, 3. drove, 4. ran, 5. swam, 6. met, 7. broke

**page 39 TENSE SENTENCE**
Answers will vary.

**page 40 MATCH THE RHYME**

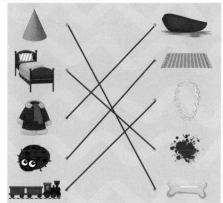

**page 41 WHAT'S THE RHYME?**

1. six, 2. hand, 3. winner, 4. gifts, 5. door, 6. page, 7. tree

**page 42 IS IT AN ADVERB?**

Yes: Sentences 2, 3 and 5
No: Sentences 1, 4 and 6

**page 43 CIRCLE THE ADVERBS**

1. happily, 2. quickly, 3. carefully, 4. daily, 5. after, 6. soon, 7. everywhere

**page 44 FILL IN THE ADVERBS**

Some possible answers: 1. quietly, 2. carefully, 3. late, 4. loudly, 5. easily, 6. beautifully, 7. happily, 8. bravely, 9. sweetly, 10. eagerly

**page 45 ADVERB SENTENCES**

Answers will vary.

**page 46 SYNONYM MATCH**

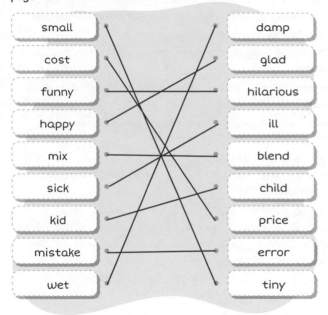

**page 47 REPLACE THE SYNONYMS**

1. Uncle Jack got me a big birthday present. 2. This looks difficult, but it is actually easy to understand. 3. The elephant is a large animal. 4. Please close the windows.

**pages 48–49 PUNCTUATION FUN**

1. ?, 2. ., 3. !, 4. ., 5. ?, 6. ., 7. !, 8. ., 9. ., 10. !, 11. ?, 12. .

Sentences will vary.

**page 50 READ AND COLOUR**

interrogative, declarative, exclamatory, imperative

**page 51 MAKE SENTENCES**

Answers will vary.

**page 52 PUNCTUATION MATCH**

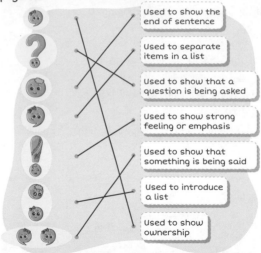

**page 53 SAYING IT RIGHT**

1. Would you like some orange juice? 2. My parents got me a ball, two pencils, a box of crayons and a bottle. 3. Ouch! The pan is hot. 4. Mom said, 'Go, give this to Grandma.'

**page 54 SINGULAR OR PLURAL?**

| box | singular | | cap | singular |
| log | singular | | eggs | plural |
| boys | plural | | monkey | singular |
| apples | plural | | lilies | plural |
| sick | singular | | shoes | plural |
| bottles | plural | | eraser | singular |
| bus | singular | | toy | singular |

**page 55 WRITE THE WORD**

1. book, books; 2. sweet, sweets; 3. circle, circles OR pie, pies; 4. snake, snakes

**pages 56–57 PLAYTIME**

Answers will vary.

**page 58 FILL THE CONJUNCTIONS**

1. and, 2. but, 3. or, 4. but, 5. or, 6. and

**page 59 JOINT SENTENCES**

Answers will vary.